MW00748797

Empty Hours

by

William E. Crocker

William E. Crocker

Memoir
BOOKS
Chico, CA

EMPTY HOURS
Copyright © 2010 by William E. Crocker
First Edition
Printed in the United States of America
Cover photo of Oregon coast

ISBN: 978-0-9793387-7-9
Library of Congress Control Number
2010929327

All rights reserved. No portion of this book
may be reproduced or reprinted in any manner
whatsoever, except in reviews, that is in
violation of copyright restrictions without the
written permission of the author.

Memoir Books
An Imprint of Heidelberg Graphics
2 Stansbury Court
Chico, California 95928

For my children and grandchildren
        To help them know the "real" me . . .

Contents

V

VI

Foreword

William Crocker is known, first, as a follower of Jesus; then, as a lover of family, an advocate for children and as a caregiver for those in need. Many other titles apply to him, but these are foremost.

He was born in Flowing Well, Saskatchewan, Canada, in 1927, as the third child in a family of ten. Though church was rarely attended, his mother (the child of missionaries to India) taught her children well. All ten grew up following Jesus and having meaningful relationships with Him.

Life was hard and Bill longed for an education. The Book of Knowledge provided his nightly bedtime reading. In his early twenties he went to the gold fields of the Yukon, and while burning magazines for warmth, he spied an ad for "opportunities in Southland colleges." He packed his gear, headed south for an education and vowed that he would "never be cold again!"

After marrying his wife, Grace, in 1954, he began his career in education — as a teacher and an elementary school administrator.

He also became the father of four children — three girls and a boy. During those years there were many attempts to write, but much was lost or scraped before it could be enjoyed by others.

In 1986, he retired from education hoping to carry out those dreams of writing and enjoying the solitude he craved. However, fate stepped in and provided him with another career, and he spent the next twenty years as an almond farmer in Northern California. Life on those eighty acres was busy and fulfilling but left little time for the writing that he longed to do. His desire to spend the rest of his years on the ranch was impossible; so he retired again.

In 2006 he settled in Chico, California, where he is busy enjoying his grandchildren, and, finally, getting back to his pen and paper where he can share his inmost feelings. He has given generously to all those around him throughout his life; and now, he shares his soul with you, his readers.

He is more than special to me; he is my life.

Grace
May 2010

Each of us writes a thousand little lines
On the pages of our minds.

The realities,
The hopes,
The dreams,
The fantasies

That each of us have
In the silence of our thoughts
Are lost forever

. . . Unless . . .

We write them down.

These are mine.

೪

I

Alone

~~~~~~

There is a place
I go alone
Where evening shadows
Stretch their arms
And welcome me
To a lonely
Paradise of solitude.

It is there
The sun lingers,
For one last glimpse,
And gently pours
Its golden vials
Upon my world
Of sweet tranquility.

Fog

～～～

I'm alone . . .
And memories,
Like soft shadows,
Steal quietly
To my mind.

I see your gentle eyes;
They pierce my soul
And trace the emptiness I feel
With you not by my side.

I feel your hands
On places they have touched
And left the "scars of gentleness"
Burning on my skin.

I hear your voice;
It comes in whispered memories
And leaves in fading echoes
Disappearing deep within.

I'm alone . . .
And treasure all the memories
You've left with me

. . . Until . . .

The fog of loneliness
Abandons me . . .
To the silence of the night.

ﷻ

Afraid

There are some thoughts
I cannot think,
Some words
I will not speak . . .
For I'm afraid
Of what they'll do.

There are some roads
I will not travel,
Some paths
I will not walk . . .
For I'm afraid
Of where they'll go.

There are some dreams
I will not dream,
Some fantasies
I will not hold . . .
For I'm afraid
Of waking up.

There are some loves
I will not share,
Some friendships
I will not make . . .
For I'm afraid
Of naught returned.

So I sit here . . .
Alone
And do not think or speak.
There are no dreams
Or fantasies;
I do not love
Or make friendships
. . . Because . . .
I am afraid.

When I'm Alone

When I'm alone,
        And thoughts of you
Steal softly 'cross
        The paths my mind has taken,
I close my eyes.
        And, silently,
I drink the fragrance
        Of your presence.

When I'm alone,
        The songs I sing
                Belong to you.
The flowers I pick
        Make your bouquet.
The castle I build
        Is for your dwelling.
The jewels I find
        Are for your adorning.

Should you never come to me,
When I'm alone,
        The songs I sing
                Will all be sad songs;

And wilted flowers
> *Will line the path to an empty house.*
The jewels I find
> *Will lie like stones that children throw.*

So, come,
Hold my hand
> *And walk with me.*
Blend your thoughts with mine.
Let our souls become as one
> *In the empty hours . . .*
>> *When I'm alone.*

Sounds of Loneliness

I heard, today,
The empty sounds
Of knocks on doors
. . . Unopened . . .
Of invitations
. . . Unaccepted . . .
Of smiles from strangers
. . . Unreturned . . .

. . . Finally . . .

I heard the sounds
Of tears that fell
On cheeks that longed
For touches from fingers
Of one who cares.

Then, I knew,
I'd heard
The sounds of loneliness.

Reality

I surrounded you
With dreams
Of loneliness
And charm,
Last night.

I caressed
Your body
With my eyes
And drank the fragrance
Of your beauty.

It seems,
That now . . .
I cling to dreams
In place of reality.

Old Ship

I feel like an old ship
Anchored in the bay,
Too old and slow
To battle storms
Or haul the freight
That pays the way.

I've had my turns
On stormy seas
And danced on waves
That threatened me.

I've spent my time
On misty isles
And slept with strangers
In lonely ports.

I've heard the songs
That nature sings
And drunk the wine
Of slower times.

. . . Now . . .

The journey's over
The mellow, harbor lights
Of yesterday
Are gone.

I'm anchored in the bay
And people come to see
This old ship
Whose memories hang,
Like shrouds of rope,
Down from the mast.

And, younger ships have come
To take my place upon the sea.

ஐ

Solitude

~~~~~~~

I spent my summer days
In solitude
And drank the wine
Of long days
And silent nights.

I read some poems,
Heard some songs,
Turned the pages
Of the past.

Often,
You came into view
And my solitude
Closed in on me.

And, like the shadows,
That become the night,
The solitude became
My loneliness.

Midnight

〜〜〜

I'm alone
Shadows move
. . . Slowly . . .
Across my mind.

Black figures
Spring up quietly
And unexpectedly
By the trees,

. . . Until . . .

My world is dark.
I feel no fear, no pain,
. . . Only awe . . .

How quickly and quietly
The little shadows
Are fused
Into total darkness . . .

And midnight comes.
৵

Real Me

Within
There is an island
Surrounded by a sea
Of loneliness.
Where waves of living
And time
Erode my soul,
Leaving bare
The shores of self.

I vacation
On that island,
Now
And then,
To feel the washing
That takes place
And see
The reality
That is me.

Isolation

〜〜〜〜〜〜

It was a little thing, at first,
That hurt our foolish pride.
But, soon, it grew
To enormous size,
'Til we could no longer hear
The words of regret.

The silence formed a chasm
Far too great
For us to cross.
So we sat in loneliness
And watched the isolation
That took place.

✍

Bridges

~~~~~~

I saw you, in the distance,
On an island
Surrounded by a sea
Of loneliness.

I called;
You answered.
And we met . . .
At a distance.

In time,
We started building bridges,
Island to island
Was our plan.

When we reached
The deepest part,
Where pillars of trust
Were needed,
We failed to find them

. . . And we stopped . . .

In the end,
All we built were piers.

And the distance between
Was far too great
For even proper farewells.

Walls

~~~~~

We worked together
And built a wall,
Brick by brick
Was laid in place

The puzzle
Of our lives
Became
That wall.

How sad it was
To discover that
We lived
On opposite sides.

Shadows

City lights
Are growing dim
As music in the hall
Slows down.
And, lovers . . .
Holding close . . .
Dance to rhythms
Of swaying shadows
On the wall.

In the streets,
I see the lonely ones
Who stand in shadows tall
And tremble . . .
From the fear . . .
Of empty rooms
And, conversations
Not returned.

Waking in San Francisco

The sun did not rise with me this morning.
The cold, grey mist was there
Embracing all the places
We had been the night before.

The music, too, was gone;
And emptiness enfolded me
Like silent fog
On city streets.

Were you ever here?
Did we sing a song
And dance in the moonlight . . .
Embrace, laugh and
Hold each other?

I cannot find you now.

Healing Tree

There is a place
I need to go
Where winds are soft
And streams are slow,
Where I can rest . . .
By the healing tree.

There are some tears
That I must shed
And bleeding I must do.
I have some wounds
That will not mend
Until I rest . . .
By the healing tree.
ﬞ

II

Are You the Door?

The union of love is complete . . .
The moment of passion is gone . . .
She lies in my arms
And tenderly,
Her fingers move across my skin.

It is then
That a greater love,
Mysteriously,
Is revealed.

Her soul
And
Mine
Mingle and move together
Like the mists and the trees by the river.

. . . Silently . . .

The fusion of spirits takes place.
In a world without words . . .
The holding
The gentle whispers
The brushing of tender lips,
Blending our souls into one.

Sweet passion,
Are you the door?

ক

One

~

God gave me
One life to live,
One heart and mind;
He provided me
With one mother,
One father,
And a path through life
Selected just for me.

. . . Then . . .

He gave me you,
My one and only,
To live that life
And walk that path with me.
He made you that
One mother
Of my children.

I have one God,
One moon, one sun, one lover.

HOW BLESSED I AM!
~

My Song

There is a happy song
I cannot sing today,
For all the thoughts of you
Were surely washed away
By swiftly flowing tears,
That mingled with the rain.

I searched the empty hallways,
And every corner of my mind,
But all the fading memories
Had left me long ago.
All I saw were shadows
Where you had been before.

I listened for your voice
In every song I heard
But all the fading echoes
Had left me long ago.
All I heard were shadows
Falling to the ground.

There is a happy song
I want to sing today,
Of sunlight mixed with shadows
And memories of you,
Of flowers, songs, and laughter . . .
All mingled with the rain.

Slow Times

I like the slow times . . .
      When all the work is done,
      And evening shadows creep
      Across the fields;
      When somber trees
      Stand still and wait . . .
          For darkness to descend.

I like the slow winds . . .
      That stir the waters
      With their playful hands,
      And send their ripples
      To bathe the tired feet
      Of giant firs, that stand . . .
          In watch along the shore.

I like the slow trains . . .
      That climb the hills
      With plaintive, lonely wails;
      And send their echoed
      Searching through the night,
      For sleepy, little towns . . .
          That lie along their paths.

I like the slow days . . .
> When all the time is mine,
> And fantasies and dreams
> Come calling on my mind;
> And anxious thoughts
> Stand still and wait . . .
>> To repossess my mind.

I like the slow walks . . .
> When evening shadows fall,
> When times we spend alone
> Are silent hours
> Of listening to our hearts
> Whispering words of love . . .
>> That only God can hear.

I like the slow times . . .
> When you are by my side.

ꙮ

Flames

The fire is hot,
The flames leap high
To light the room
And warm the lovers . . .
Swaying with the shadows
On the wall.

They dance to rhythms
Of music scarcely heard,
Forgetting the hour . . .
And the embers
Slowly dying.

. . . Until . . .

The shadows leave them,
Alone,
In the darkness,
With each other . . .
Who they cannot see.

Carefully, they fan the spark,
Among the ashes cold,
And hope . . .
The hearth will once again
Be bright.

And, from the fire,
Burning deep within,
They reach out
And touch . . .
In silence.

&

Now

When I see the dreams,
Of yesterday,
Float by like clouds
I stop . . .
Reach out . . .
And hold them . . .
To my melancholy heart.

One by one
They disappear,
Like sand I clutched . . .
When I was young.
Leaving me with nothing
. . . But . . .
An empty shell.

. . . And, then . . .

I come to now,
When you are at my side,
And pleasure possesses me . . .
Until I cry.

Our Burden

~~~~~~~~~

The time we spent together
Is but a frozen moment in memory
Of the two of us
. . . Alone . . .
. . . Unseen . . .
But by God.

No one knows what joys,
What ecstasies, we felt
As we traced the sadness down . . .
And left it
By the path
. . . Forgotten . . .

Until the morning rays of light revealed,
In each of us,
The emptiness of that drifting moment,
. . . Already gone . . .

And we found the sadness
We'd put down,
To carry it once more
. . . A greater burden . . .

She Was Special

She was special
For such a long, long time . . .
I knew her ways,
Her hidden thoughts,
She left me no surprises
. . . Until . . .
She was gone.

It was my love for her.

I missed . . .
The touch of hand and soul,
The sleeping – and the waking,
The laughing – and the crying,

. . . But, most of all . . .

I missed the quiet times
When soul touched soul
And eyes spoke
Quietly and softly,
Until the heart of love was filled,
And spilled in tears,
Like gentle rain.

The message of love was there
Without the noise of words.
And the touching of our hands

Revealed . . .

The fullness of our love.

&

At the Airport

~~~~~~~~~~~~~~~~

She left him for awhile
And it seemed alright

. . . Until . . .

The sound
And touch of her
Was gone.

He failed to sleep
And the hunger disappeared.

He could not feel the soft caresses
Of places only God can see.
And emptiness,
Like soft shadows,
Moved within his soul

. . . Then, he knew . . .

His love was gone.

ᘔ

You Came

Before you came,
    I lived contented
        In my world.
I shared my time
    With friends
And gave them gifts . . .
    Of me.
I tried to touch
    Each life
        That passed my way.

But, when you came . . .
    My world
        Was changed.
I gave my time
    And gifts
        To only you . . .
And seldom knew
    Who passed my way.

Parting

~~~~

We should not part
When clouds appear
Casting shadows on our path.

We should not part
When troubles come
And darken our world.

We should not part
When money is gone
And times are really hard.

We should not part
When years have past
And eyes have grown dim.

We should not part
When kids are gone
And emptiness fills our abode.

We should not part
When trials o'erpower
And all our friends have gone.

We should stay together,
As we vowed,
"'Til death do us part."

I Can Dream

~~~~~~

If I could sing,
I'd sing the sweetest
Melodies for you.

If I could paint,
I'd paint the greatest
Scenes for you.

If I could write,
I'd write the wildest
Poems for you.

If I could dance,
I'd dance across
The skies for you.

. . . Now . . .

I can dream,
And, the dreams I dream
Are all of you!

M-M-M-M-M-M!

~

III

Reunion

When you go back
To places in the past,
And search for friends
You left behind. . .
You will not find them.

Like you, time and space
Have taken then away
From yesterday . . .
That misty isle
That floats in memory.

From the puzzle,
Each took a piece . . .
And changed it.

. . . And, now . . .

The pieces do not fit;
And the picture that is made
Is one you never knew.

Thanks, Dad

Thanks, Dad,
For walking slow
In hurried times,
For playing games
When work was prime,
For losing fights
When you were strong,
For standing fast,
When I was wrong,
For running slow
When I was small,
For helping me
When I would fall,
For kneeling down
Before our God,

. . . But, most of all . . .
For loving Mom.

Thanks, Dad.

Little Feet

~~~~~~~~~~

I wonder where
The little feet have gone,
That followed me
When I was strong.

It was so easy then
To lead the way,
And conquer worlds
Beyond their yards.
They'd embark on any trail
And trust me as their guide.

. . . But, now . . .

They've gone ahead
On paths I've never been;
And I'm too old and slow
To follow them.

I wonder where
The little feet will go.

ஐ

Mi Amiga

I walked with you
For just one mile today.
I felt the joy
Of reaching out
And the touching
Of our hands
I heard a sweet song
In every word you spoke,
And clearly understood
The message of your heart.

When I walked with you;
I never saw the hills we climbed,
Or felt the many rocks
Beneath my tired feet.
Your awesome burden
Seemed so light
When added unto mine.

I only saw the flowers
Reflected in your eyes
And felt the velvet
Of your touch
While pleasure soon became
The destination of my path.

. . . Now . . .

Our walk has ended;
The empty path seems wide,
The weeds, the dust, and rocks
Crowd every step I take

. . . Until . . .

I think of you
And the mile we walked today.
ے

Elizabeth—in the Lobby

You're so young
To be alone,
With big eyes
That never smile
And brown hair
All tumbling down . . .
Like waterfalls
That I have seen.

You're so fortunate
To be alone,
With good choices
Lined up "by the mile,"
And handsome men
All tumbling down . . .
Like football stars
That I have seen.

Be so careful,
When you're alone,
Or bright futures,
Worth their while,
And handsome men
Will tumble down . . .
Like dominoes
That I have seen.

Your Waiter

~~~~~~~

With kind eyes
And gentle soul,
You brought
Flowers,
Soft words,
And sweet touches . . .
To my table.

You filled my empty heart
And hungry spirit.
You brightened
My drab and lonely world.
You touched
The hurting places . . .
At my table.

. . . Now . . .

With sad eyes
And silent words,
You come to me.

My friend,
I'm filled and strong,
Let me
Your waiter be.

∾

Smiles

~~~~~~~~

They sit
At little desks,
With eyes
That follow mine,
And wait
For signs from me
To show them
How to feel.

I hesitate in silence,

. . . Then . . .
I smile.

And thirty little faces
Reflect the light
I feel within.

ও

Fast Friend

I saw him in my office,
He seemed so small.
His eyes were large and sad.
His name was Pete.
His mother said that he was "slow."

His sister, Sissy, she was "great:"
The lead in the Christmas play,
The best pianist in school,
A "straight A" student,
A great helper around the house,
A true gem!

But, Pete was slow,
A handful who needed to be watched.
They'd had him tested, to make sure.
Pete's eyes were troubled;
His daddy knew he wasn't slow.
He could outrun the fastest,
And, outsmart the smartest on the block.
But, then . . . his daddy was gone
And his momma didn't know.

I took them to their classrooms . . .
"This is Sissy; you are lucky.
Put her with the best,
For she is tops in everything."

Let me take Pete by myself.
We stopped along the way and talked.
"I'm Mr. C, and I know
You're fast like me.
I also know you're smart.
Do you like to hike?"

We made a bargain to be friends.
He promised to bring me samples of his work . . .
This would prove that he was smart.
And, I would race him once a day . . .
This would prove that he was fast.

"Miss T., this is Pete
He's my friend,
I will see him once a day.
He's fast and smart;
Please help him stay that way."

To prove that he was fast . . .
He ran the children down.
He brought me terrible work . . .
To show me he was smart.
But, he learned to be the boss . . .
To make the letters stay on lines
And numbers to correctly add.
His strength and speed he did control . . .
After sitting on the bench.

Each day he came and leaned on me.
We talked and laughed
And sometimes cried.

He learned to be wise and strong.
He became a MAN,
With heart and soul,

And helped his sister . . .
Who fell down.

To Know Love

~~~~~~~~~~~~~~

A child's love for a parent
Is the closest to God's love
That can be found.

It tolerates . . .
Rejection,
Abuse,
Neglect,
And, even, hatred.
It is forgiving,
It carries no grudges.

A child will accept any excuse,
Any glimmer of hope,
Any sign of love,
And make believe that
The Mom or Dad he knows
Is the "Best in the World."

With every rejection,
Every harsh word,
Every abuse,
The child's love deepens.

He will lie,
Steal,
Fight,
And defy the greatest authority
To protect his Mom or Dad.
Years of absence
Only intensify that love.

To know love . . .
Become as a child.

ﻌ

Silent Times

Stay awhile . . .
Your eyes are sad,
I've talked too much
And never heard
     The silence of your words.

The sadness of you laughter
Escaped me for a time
    . . . But, now . . .
I see the aching of your heart
Reflected in
     The absence of your words.

Come, sit beside me,
And let me make amends.
I cannot let you go
Before we've had
     Our silent times

We Met

I met you just today,
At an unexpected time,
And we talked.

I shared with you today,
Sweet memories of joy,
And we laughed.

I walked with you today,
On crowded streets,
And we rested.

I wined with you today,
Dark eyes across the table,
And we touched.

I left you just today,
'Twas the sweetest farewell,
And we parted.

I remembered you today,
Soft eyes in the sunset,
And I cried.

IV

The Sign

I was sad today.
I looked at my burned-out life
And saw so much wasted time . . .
Time spent in "making a living."
I saw no great victories for God,
No great deeds for mankind.

I saw a burned-out life,
Standing alone,
And useless,
With very little future.

I remembered a sign,
Hanging on a wall
In a temporary dwelling.
It was on a charred piece of wood,
Taken from a fire-ravaged house.
Painted on it were the words,
"GOD LOVES YOU."

God, take my burned-out life,
And paint on a piece of it,
"GOD LOVES YOU."
Let me hang it on my temporary dwelling
So that others may see your love.

Restoration

〰〰〰〰〰

Walls built on walls,
Temple over temple,
Cities built to last,
Read about their past.
Crumbling stones
Mingled with the ashes
Tell their story . . .
Civilization ended.

. . . Now . . .
A sign on a cathedral,

"YOUR DONATIONS ARE NEEDED
FOR THE RESTORATION
OF THIS TEMPLE."

Plans built on plans,
A life built for success,
Achievement after achievement;
Shattered dreams
Mingled with despair;
Lost on that journey,
See the fallen star;
Future suspended.

. . . Now . . .
A sign on my heart, for God,

**"YOUR PRESENCE IS NEEDED
FOR THE RESTORATION
OF MY SOUL"**

&

Ownership

Why do we buy the land,
Throw up a fence,
And call it our own?

I have never yet
Seen one Deed of Trust
Signed by God.

We own nothing . . .
Not the air,
The water
Or the soil.
We merely rent it . . .
From Him.

I would like to avoid
The claim of ownership
To anything.
Especially,
If its made by man . . .
For surely,
It will break.

Just give me health,
Love of peace
Gentleness of spirit,
Courage to take a stand,
And, above all,
Wisdom.

. . . For then . . .

I will give all things away . . .
Before they're taken from me.

God, Are You Aware?

God, are you aware of what man
Has done to this creation of yours?
Have you seen the hills he's flattened,
And the rivers he has dammed?
Oh, God!
Are you asleep?

Man has made the paths into freeways,
Dark places light . . .
Light places dark.
The silent places by the sea
Have become cities of noise
That drown out the beat of the waves
And hide the light of the stars.
Oh, God!
Are you aware?

Have you seen the forests on the hillside?
The trees . . .
Now in rows.
The lonely place
By the mountains and stream,
Where my soul would search for you,
Is now a park for thousands
Who defile your handiwork?
Oh, God!
Do you care?

Have you seen the deserts
Where you came to pray?
Now the tanks of war ply to and fro
And armies of men search for oil.
There are no winding streams . . .
Only straight aqueducts.
The place of secret prayer
Is, now, by millions seen.
Oh, God!
Don't you weep?

Oh, God!
Its hard for my ears to hear
When the engines roar . . .
And never stop.
Its hard for my eyes to see
With the smoke and dust . . .
That never settle.
And my heart cannot feel your touch;
For there are no lonely, silent places left.

Oh, God!
I'm sorry!
I know you care,
For you cannot sleep
With all this din.
You are aware
Of the lonely heart's plight.
You must shed tears
To see us so lost . . .
. . . Trying to improve . . .
On paradise.

I Shall Not Want

~~~~~~~~~~~~~~

You've confused
Your wants
With your needs.

. . . Remember the difference . . .

Needs were created
By God;
Wants are made
Solely by you.

"The Lord is my Shepherd,
I shall not want."

ও

V

Fickle Lover

The remorseful ocean murmurs her regrets
For the fierce tantrum
She had thrown the night before.
She unfolds her pleated skirt
Along the shore,
And whispers, "Come."

She has seduced me before,
And is trying again.
Her tide's long arms
Wrap lovingly around the rocks
And lavish wet kisses
On their craggy faces.

I hold her in my heart
And dance with joy
On the sun-drenched sand.
She is a fickle lover
Who ever toys with my heart
And draws me
Down to the sea again.

Searching

When I was young,
I searched . . .
For little things,
Like frogs and eagles' nests.

When I grew up,
I searched . . .
For pots of gold
And the very best.

Now, I'm old,
And, I search . . .
For the meaning of life
And a little rest.

Modern Poetry

The words lie together
Like shattered slivers of glass,
Swept high
Into some forgotten corner.

They do not resemble
Art, or cups, or vases,
Or anything I know.
Nor do they hold
The wine of understanding.

They do, however,
Reveal the confusion
Of their conflicted
Creators' minds!

VI

Emptiness

〰️

The sun did not rise
With me this morning.

The cold, grey mist
Was there . . .
Chilling all the places
We had been
The night before.

I could not see
The paths we'd walked
Or places where
We'd stopped.

I only felt
The cold mist's arms
About my soul

. . . And . . .

Emptiness.

ꝏ

Forgetting

Too many days of rain,
Cold winds
And silence;

Too many nights of staying
In places
I don't belong;

Too many hours of waiting
For the one
Who won't return.

Too many dreams
Of tomorrows
Filled with love;

Too many broken plans
Of leaving
And not returning;

Too many times of hurting,
Of sad songs,
And loneliness.

When the sun returns,
I'm leaving . . .
And, I'll forget this place.

Regrets

There was a time
I wanted you
So badly
It hurt . . .
Deep within.

. . . Then . . .

After the hurting
And wanting stopped,
You came
To me.

. . . Now . . .

I wonder why
I ever felt
The need
To have you.

For I look at you
And feel sorry
That you ever came
To me.

Open Door

You left an open door,
And a stranger wandered in;
She straightened out
The cluttered rooms
And mended broken things.

She wiped away the dust
And stains from many tears;
She brought flowers, soft music
And candles for light.

. . . And . . .

I closed the door.

Departure

～～～

Written on the death of my father-in-law, Lawrence T. Holman, Sr. Larry was a retired minister, creative photographer, and a friend to all.

At your birth,
You cried;
And they rejoiced.

In between
The coming and the going,
You left some bridges
That you built,
Some flowers along
The paths you walked,
And songs
Whose echoes will not fade.

. . . Now . . .

At your departure,
They cry;
And, I wonder,
Do you rejoice?

～

A Song She Might Have Sung

Written for my sister-in-law, Jan Moore, on the morning of January 3, 1998, (the day she went to be with Jesus.) Suffering from ALS (Lou Gehrig's disease,) Jan was unable to speak, but nodded in agreement with the sentiment.

Please, turn the music down
And keep your voices low;
There's a new song I'm hearing now
In a voice that's soft and clear;
It's the One who's always been with me . . .
He's walking closer now.

I've lost all things I've ever owned;
I cannot bring Him gifts
Or sing His praises now.
I have no strength to do great deeds;
I stand before Him . . . empty.

What does a Saviour, such as mine,
Need of earthly things?
The whole wide universe is His.
Or what great deeds
Or songs from me
Compare to those the angels sing?

So like a child,
I lift my emptiness
And bring Him only praise.
I lift my soul, and wait
For Him to cradle me
In His eternal, loving arms.

Shhhh . . . hush your voices;
Keep the music down.
The One who's always been with me
Is walking closer now.

≈

Exit

~~~

Keep me close
For time is running out,
I've moved
Too far . . .
Too fast . . .
In the corridors of time.

. . . Swiftly . . .

I've run by the side roads
Leading to slow and easy times.

I've picked no flowers
Along the streams and paths,
Wasted no time
On songs
And tales
Of travelers along the way.

The moments . . .
The hours . . .
The days . . .
The "glittering coins of time,"
I've spent without a thought.
The purse will soon be empty.

. . . The "EXIT" sign looms large . . .

And grins
Above the door
That opens up its arms to fold me

. . . Softly . . .

Into night's dark bosom.
✢

I Must Go

~~~~~~~~~~~

The time is now
That I must go . . .

I hear the distant sound
Of lonely trains . . .
You cannot hear.

I see the horizon
Full of dreams . . .
You cannot see.

I want to chase the wandering wind
And follow dreams.
You want to stay and watch the fire
Burn and die.

I must loose the chains that hold me
And bid farewell . . .

I may not come this way again.

The time is now
That I must go.

ℒ

Breinigsville, PA USA
06 June 2010
239242BV00001B/3/P